TO

FROM

the dash

MAKING A DIFFERENCE WITH YOUR LIFE FROM BEGINNING TO END

LINDA ELLIS | MAC ANDERSON

THOMAS NELSON
Since 1798

NASHVILLE DALLAS MEXICO CITY RIO DE JANEIRO

Dedicated to the life of John William Hicks,

the dash between June 12, 1930–July 5, 2004.

Dad, I'll love you forever.

Linda

The Dash

Published in Nashville, Tennessee, by Thomas Nelson. Thomas Nelson is a registered trademark of Thomas Nelson, Inc.

Originally published by Simple Truths LLC
1952 McDowell Road, Suite 300
Naperville, IL 60563
Toll Free: 800.900.3427
www.simpletruths.com

This edition published under license from Simple Truths exclusively for Thomas Nelson Inc.

Thomas Nelson, Inc., titles may be purchased in bulk for educational, business, fund-raising, or sales promotional use. For information, please e-mail SpecialMarkets@ThomasNelson.com.

ISBN-13: 978-1-4003-1998-5

Printed in Singapore

12 13 14 15 16 TWP 6 5 4 3 2 1

www.thomasnelson.com

Contents

Introduction

The letter hit my desk on June 10, 2003. I opened it to see a short handwritten note attached to a single sheet of paper. The note was from Anna Lee Wilson, a Successories franchisee from Evansville, Indiana. She thanked me for speaking the week before at the grand opening of her new restaurant, and at the bottom of the note was a postscript that read: "I know you enjoy inspirational poems, and this is my all-time favorite. It's titled 'The Dash,' by Linda Ellis." When Anna Lee speaks, I listen because she is one of the kindest, most caring people I've ever met. I knew that if it was her favorite, it had to be good.

I can count on one hand the number of times I've read something that stopped me in my tracks, words that bypassed the brain and went straight to the heart. This was one of those moments. It was one of those times when I immediately thought, *How can I use my talents to share these powerful, thought-provoking words with the rest of the world?*

The first step was to contact the author, Linda Ellis. She answered the phone, and I introduced myself and told her how much I loved her poem. She then told me her story, how one afternoon in 1996 she was inspired to write "The Dash." Her life, she said, had not been the same since.

Life works in strange ways. I feel that this project was meant to be. Joseph Epstein wrote, "We do not choose to be born. We do not choose our parents . . . or the country of our birth. . . . We do not, most of us, choose to die; nor do we choose the time and conditions of our death. But within this realm of choicelessness, we do choose how we live."[1]

That's what this book is all about.

Read it! Enjoy it! And just one more thing—make someone's day by sharing it.

Mac Anderson

Founder, Successories and Simple Truths

the dash
by LINDA ELLIS

I read of a man who stood to speak

at the funeral of a friend.

He referred to the dates on her tombstone

from the beginning . . . to the end.

He noted that first came the date of her birth

and spoke of the following date with tears,

but he said what mattered most of all

was the dash between those years.

For that dash represents all the time

that she spent alive on earth,

and now only those who loved her

know what that little line is worth.

BERNARD
SWF

For it matters not how much we own,

the cars . . . the house . . . the cash.

What matters most is how we live and love

and how we spend our dash.

So think about this long and hard;

are there things you'd like to change?

For you never know how much time is left

that can still be rearranged.

If we could just slow down enough

to consider what's true and real

and always try to understand

the way other people feel.

I love you...

And be less quick to anger

and show appreciation more

and love the people in our lives . . .

like we've never loved before.

If we treat each other with respect

and more often wear a smile . . .

remembering that this special dash

might only last a little while.

So when your eulogy is being read,

with your life's actions to rehash,

would you be proud of the things they say

about how you spent your dash?

How Will You Spend Your Dash?

One of the most difficult lessons in life is that less is often more. Only as I've grown older have I "gotten it." Focusing on your most important priorities and continually removing the clutter is key to any true success in life. That's what I love about this poem. In less than 250 words, it captures the simple truths of why we were put on this earth.

When you look through the lens of a camera, sometimes the image is blurred. However, with one small tweak of the lens, it can become crystal clear. For me, that's what happens when beautiful photography is combined with inspirational words—it can resonate with your imagination and bring the idea to life.

Within the words of this beautiful poem, I discovered a few simple truths that can make a difference in any life. I'd like to share them with you to help bring the goals for your "dash" into focus.

Mac Anderson

Slow Down

If we could just slow down enough
to consider what's true and real . . .

The maxim is true: "We don't remember days; we remember moments." At today's hectic pace, we often forget to savor small pleasures while we make big plans.

In the race to be better or best, we sometimes lose sight of just *being*. And just being, just soaking in and relishing a beautiful moment, can provide some of life's greatest delights. A crackling fire on a cold winter night, a good book, a love letter from your spouse, a spectacular sunset, a great meal, a timeless moment with your child or a friend . . . These moments, if we stop long enough to enjoy them, are the essence of life.

I love to fish, especially for largemouth bass. Several years ago, I was watching television late one night and got this crazy notion to go fishing in the lake behind my house—at that moment. Of course, my wife thought

I was nuts. It was almost midnight! I convinced her I was sane and took off. I slipped out the door to a warm summer breeze and looked up at the starry sky and breathtaking full moon. I allowed my senses to soak in every second—the sweet smell of honeysuckle, the sound of every cricket and bullfrog, the moon's reflection dancing off the water—it was a perfect night.

After walking across a small field, I took out a flashlight and selected a lure. On my first cast, I reeled in a bass that weighed over five pounds, one of the largest I had ever caught! I gently released it back into the water and continued my midnight adventure. During the next two hours, I caught seventeen bass, all between two and five pounds. Although I've fished for almost fifty years, no fishing experience has topped that warm summer night.

But that night provided far more than a spectacular fishing memory. It was a life memory. It provided me a snapshot of what life could be like if I just slowed down enough to savor the moments. On my way back to the house, as I walked through the tall grass, I took one last look at the sky and stopped to say, "Thank You, God, for giving me this night."

Remember, life will last only a little while. . . . So savor the moments, savor the memories, of *your* Dash.

Rejoice in the Lord, and your bones will flourish . . .

and your cheeks will glow. . . .

Joy is balm and healing,

and if you will but rejoice,

God will give power.

A. B. SIMPSON

True and Real

If we could just slow down enough to consider what's true and real . . .

Knowing yourself, finding your true purpose in life, is the essence of *true* and *real.* You have to be, before you do, to have lasting inner peace. In other words, making a living is not the same as making a life. Find what makes your heart sing, and create your own music.

Many people work all their lives and dislike what they do for a living. In fact, a 2010 *CBS News* poll revealed that more than 50 percent of people in the American workplace are unhappy with their jobs. Loving what you do is one of the most important keys to living a true and real Dash.

You can't fake passion. It is the fuel that drives any dream and makes you happy to be alive. However, the first step to loving what you do is to self-analyze, to simply know what you love. We all have unique talents and interests, and one of life's greatest challenges is to match these talents with career opportunities that bring out the best in us. It's not easy, and sometimes we are able to find it only through trial and error—but it's worth the effort.

Ray Kroc, for example, discovered his passion when he had the vision to franchise the first McDonald's at the age of fifty-two. He never "worked" another day of his life.

John James Audubon was unsuccessful for most of his life. He was a terrible businessman. No matter how many times he changed locations, changed partners, or changed businesses, he still failed miserably. Not until he understood that he must change himself did he have any shot at success.

And what changes did Audubon make? He followed his passion. He had always loved the outdoors and was an excellent hunter. In addition, he was a good artist and, as a hobby, would draw local birds.

Once he stopped trying to be a businessman and started doing what he loved to do, his life turned around. He traveled the country observing and drawing birds, and his art was ultimately collected in a book titled *Birds of America*. The book earned him a place in history as one of the greatest wildlife artists ever. But more important, the work made him happy and provided the peace of mind he'd been seeking all his life. An intentional pursuit of your passion reflects what your Dash is truly all about.

"For I know the plans I have for you,"
declares the Lord, "plans to prosper you
and not to harm you,
plans to give you hope and a future."

JEREMIAH 29:11

Feelings

And always try to understand the way other people feel.

I once heard someone say, “If you teach your children the Golden Rule, you will have left them an estate of incalculable value.” Truer words were never spoken.

More than anything, the Golden Rule is about kindness—the universal language, understood by all. John Blumberg, author, speaker, and friend, recently told me a story I'd like to share with you:

I had just experienced a pleasant flight from New York back to Chicago on United Airlines. It was one of those days when almost everything had gone right. That's until I exited the tram to the airport's economy parking lot and realized that I had lost my wallet on my homeward journey.

Throughout the drive home, I mentally retraced my steps. Once home, I placed calls to the lost-and-found at O'Hare and LaGuardia and to United and the TSA in New York. At that late-night hour I got recordings, so I left each a detailed message. I then went to bed, knowing I had done all I could do. I fell asleep thinking of the hassle of replacing everything in the wallet.

The next morning, I had been up for less than an hour when a man called. Bob identified himself as an employee with United Airlines, and his question was music to my ears: "Mr. Blumberg, are you missing a wallet?" Relieved and grateful, I thanked him for returning my call to United's lost-and-found.

But Bob didn't know about that call. He wasn't with the lost-and-found department—nor was it his job to personally follow up with passengers who had left their belongings on the airplane. He was the night mechanic and had simply found the wallet on my seat. My phone number was not anywhere in my wallet, so I immediately knew that he had taken extra effort to track down my home phone number. But that effort was only the beginning.

Bob had waited to call until the next morning, assuming I would be sleeping. He told me he was leaving work at 7:00 a.m. and wondered if I would be home so he could deliver my wallet to my house on his way home. After talking logistics for a minute, I realized that he was going over an hour out of his way. But he insisted. I finally got him to agree that I would immediately leave my house and meet him partway, in a direction near his home. For the next forty-five minutes, we both drove toward a common meeting place.

We finally met in the parking lot of a commercial building. As I got out of my car to meet this stranger-turned-hero, I introduced myself to Bob. He sported a heavy United Airlines uniform coat made necessary by the cold December morning. He greeted me with a big smile and handed me my wallet. I pulled some cash from my pocket to give him a sizable tip for all his efforts. As I reached to hand him the cash, he didn't miss a beat.

"Absolutely not!" he said. "I have lost my wallet before," Bob continued, "and I know it is a hassle. I'm just glad I could get it back to you."

Feeling the need to *somehow* respond to his kindness, I offered the tip a couple more times. But he wouldn't budge. Realizing that my efforts to tip minimized his graciousness, I just smiled and said, "I guess I'll just have to pay it forward to someone else."

He smiled. "That would be great."

You see, Bob went the extra mile . . . and then some. He didn't do it for gain; he did it simply because it's who he is.[2]

During our Dash on this earth, we all have countless opportunities to perform unexpected acts of kindness. Washington Irving said it well: "How truly is a kind heart a fountain of gladness, making everything in its vicinity to freshen into smiles."

Have you had a kindness shown?

Pass it on. . . .

Let it travel down the years,

let it wipe another's tears,

till in heaven the deed appears.

Pass it on.

HENRY BURTON

Forgiveness

And be less quick to anger . . .

Our emotions are powerful motivators, and more than almost anything else in our lives, they will drive our behavior. Sometimes our greatest challenge is to get inside our own heads to understand what makes us tick. Why do we feel and behave the way we do?

I know two family members who were the best of friends, but several years ago, one reminded the other of something that had happened thirty years earlier. One thing led to another, and you know what? They haven't spoken since.

William Arthur Ward identified the cure with these powerful words: "Forgiveness is the key that unlocks the door of resentment and the handcuffs of hate." I know from personal experience that forgiveness works. A few times in my life I've been greatly wronged and taken advantage of. My first reaction, of course, was anger and resentment. I held it for a while and felt my stomach tie up in knots, my appetite wane, and the joy slip out of my life.

The quote from Ward provided the wake-up call I needed to forgive the person who had wronged me. It was as if I had been playing the first half of a basketball game while wearing three-pound steel shoes on each foot and in the locker room the coach said, "Mac, try these new Nike shoes in the second half." Multiply that by ten, and you'll understand how great it feels to unload your emotional weights through the power of forgiveness.

Life is too short to stay angry . . . even for a day.
Just remember that
"this special Dash
might only last a little while."

Forgiveness does not change the past,

but it does enlarge the future.

PAUL BOESE

And show appreciation more . . .

Barbara Glanz is a speaker and author and is also a good friend. One of her favorite quotes from Albert Schweitzer is: "Sometimes our light goes out but is blown again into flame by an encounter with another human being. Each of us owes the deepest thanks to those who have rekindled this inner light."[3]

When Barbara speaks, she will ask her audience to shut their eyes and think about someone who at some time in their lives has rekindled their inner light. She will leave the room in silence for several minutes. It is always a profound experience for everyone as they remember the joy they felt as they appreciate someone who was there when they needed it most.

Afterward, she'll ask them to write down the name of the person they thought of and to commit to their own act of appreciation by letting that person know in the next seventy-two hours that they thought of them. She'll suggest a phone call, a note, or even just a little prayer if they are no longer alive.

After one very moving session, a gentleman came up to talk with Barbara and thank her for creating a new awareness in him. He said he had thought of his eighth-grade literature teacher because she was everyone's favorite teacher and had really made a difference in all of their lives, and he was going to track her down and let her know what happened.

One afternoon nearly two and a half months later, Barbara received a call from him. He was very emotional and could hardly get through his story. He said that it had taken him nearly two months to track his teacher down. When he finally found her, he wrote to her, and the following week he received this letter:

Dear John,

You will never know how much your letter meant to me. I am eighty-three years old, and I am living all alone in one room. My friends are all gone. My family's gone.

I taught for fifty years, and yours is the first "thank you" letter I have ever gotten from a student. Sometimes I wonder what I did with my life. I will read and reread your letter until the day I die.

He sobbed on the phone. "Every reunion we've had, she is always the one we talked about," he said. "She was everyone's favorite teacher—we loved her!"

But no one had ever told her . . . until she received his letter.[4]

Never forget—it is not the things you get but the hearts you touch that will determine your success in your Dash.

I would maintain that thanks are the highest form of thought; and that gratitude is happiness doubled by wonder.

G. K. CHESTERTON

And love the people in our lives like we've never loved before.

I recently had dinner with someone who told me that one of his best friends had been killed in a private plane crash. Something had happened at the memorial service that he would never forget. He shared the story with me.

At the service, his friend's wife walked to the podium to speak to the gathering. She said a friend had asked her the best memory she had of their life together. At the moment, she had been too grief stricken to answer, but she had thought about it since and wanted to answer the question.

They were in their late forties when he died, and she began talking about a time in their life almost twenty years earlier. She had quit her job to obtain her master's degree, and her husband never wavered in his support.

He held down his own job and also did the cooking, cleaning, and other household chores while she studied for her degree.

One time they both stayed up all night. She was finishing her thesis, and he was preparing for an important business meeting. That morning, she walked out on their upstairs loft, looked at him over the railing, and thought about just how much she loved him. She knew how important this meeting was to his career, and she was feeling guilty that she hadn't even had time to make his breakfast. He grabbed his briefcase and hurried out. She heard the garage door open and close, but much to her surprise, she heard it open again about thirty seconds later. From above, she watched her husband dash into the house and walk over to the neglected coffee table. Tracing his finger through the dust, he wrote the words "I love you." Then he raced back to his car.

The new widow then looked out at her audience and said, "John and I had a wonderful life together. We have been around the world several times, we've had everything money can buy . . . but nothing comes close to that moment."

Our Dash moves with lightning speed. It feels like yesterday that I graduated from college . . . and now decades have passed. Although I'm very proud of my business accomplishments, in the end my life comes back to loving and being loved. Embrace every opportunity you have to love the people in your life!

Love from the center of who you are . . .
hold on for dear life to good.

ROMANS 12:9 MSG

If we treat each other with respect . . .

I was in the Oklahoma City airport when I saw a woman walking along with three little girls. They were skipping and singing, "Daddy's coming home on a big jet! Daddy's coming home on a big jet!" All excited! Eyes lit up like diamonds! Wild anticipation! They had never before met Daddy coming home on a jet. Their mother was so proud of them and their enthusiasm. You could see it in her eyes.

Then the plane arrived, the door opened, and the passengers streamed in. You didn't have to ask which one was Daddy. The girls' bright eyes were glued on him. But his first look was for his wife and seeing her, he yelled, "Why didn't you bring my top coat?" and walked right past his adoring daughters. Here was a man who had an opportunity to be great, and he didn't recognize it.

I heard Charlie Cullen tell that story forty years ago, and I have never forgotten it.

How many times a day, a week, a month do we have the opportunity to be great through simple acts of kindness? In your Dash, never underestimate the power of a touch, a smile, a kind word, a listening ear, or an honest compliment. We all have the potential to turn a life around.

DO NOTHING

out of selfish ambition

or vain conceit,

but in humility consider others

better than yourselves.

PHILIPPIANS 2:3

Smile

And more often wear a smile.

Our Dash is short, but it can be wide . . .

A bellhop made my day recently. After checking into an Atlanta hotel, Sam (his name was on his badge) picked up my two bags, gave me a big smile, and said, "Isn't it a gorgeous day today?"

I nodded. "Sure is."

He then said, "I just spent the entire weekend with my two grandkids, and I can't remember when I've had more fun. Aren't kids great?"

"Sam," I said, "it seems like you're having a great day."

He then looked up with a grin I'll never forget. "Mr. Anderson, every day above ground is a great day!"

I walked into my room feeling recharged by Sam's enthusiasm. It was obvious that he had chosen to live life to the fullest, and my bet is that if given the opportunity to touch someone's life in a positive way, he took it every time.

Every day, we have that same opportunity to make a positive difference in the lives of others. We can choose to mope about our lot in life, or we can decide to live in awe, touching hearts along the way.

Ah, yes . . . we all know ducks who make lots of noise, quacking and complaining about their problems in life. And then there are eagles, who go about their business and consistently soar above the crowd.

Thanks, Sam, for soaring into my life.

The pleasantest things in the world are pleasant thoughts,

and the great art of life is

to have as many of them as possible.

MICHEL DE MONTAIGNE

Change

So think about this long and hard;
are there things you'd like to change?

Over a century ago, William James, one of the founders of modern psychology, said, "The great discovery of this generation is that a human being can alter their life by altering their attitude." Each day, we wake up in the morning, we choose our clothes, we choose our breakfast, but most importantly, we choose our attitude.

One of the most wonderful things about having a positive attitude is the number of people it touches, many times in ways you'll never know.

In my book *The Power of Attitude*, I tell a story about going to a convenience store to get a newspaper and a pack of gum. The young woman at the checkout counter said, "That'll be five dollars, please."

As I reached into my wallet, the thought occurred to me that a newspaper and gum didn't quite make it to five dollars. When I looked up to get a "requote," she had a big smile on her face and said, "Gotcha! I gotta get my tip in there somehow!"

I laughed when I realized I'd been had.

She then glanced down at the paper I was buying. "I'm sick and tired of all this negative stuff on the front pages. I want to read some good news for a change." She then said, "In fact, I think someone should publish a Good News newspaper—a paper with wonderful, inspiring stories about people overcoming adversity and doing good things for others. I'd buy one every day!" She then thanked me for coming in and laughed. "Maybe we'll get lucky tomorrow; maybe we'll get some good news!" She made my day.

The following day, after my business appointments, I dropped by the same store again to pick up bottled water, but a different young lady was behind the counter. As I checked out I said, "Good afternoon," and handed her money for the water. She said nothing. Not a word, not a smile . . . nothing. She just handed me my change and in a negative tone ordered, "Next!"

It hit me right between the eyes: two people, same age; one made me feel great, and the other, well, made me feel that I had inconvenienced her by showing up.

By the choices we make, by the attitudes we exhibit, we are influencing lives every day in positive or negative ways . . . our family, our peers, our friends, and even strangers we've never met before and will never see again. So when you brush your teeth every morning, look in the mirror and ask your self, *Are there things I'd like to change?* How will you choose to live your Dash—as the grouch or as the "good-news girl"? Your answer will go a long way toward determining the joy and happiness you will experience in your life.

Our days are a kaleidoscope.
Every instant a change takes place.
New harmonies, new contrasts,
new combinations of every sort.

The most familiar people stand each moment in some new relation to each other, to their work, to surrounding objects.

HENRY WARD BEECHER

Making a Difference

What matters is how we live and love and how we spend our dash . . .

It's not the things we get but the hearts we touch that will determine our success in life. Making a difference in the lives of others is what the Dash is all about. In the end, however, the significance of our life will be determined by the choices we make. We can choose positive over negative, smiles over frowns, giving over taking, and love over hate. It is only when we take responsibility for our choices that we begin to realize we truly are the masters of our destiny. Only then will our lives begin to change for the better.

One of the most powerful stories about choices that I've ever read was written by Lance Wubbels in a book we coauthored called *To a Child, Love Is Spelled T-I-M-E*. In January 2003, I sent the title to Lance as a possible gift book idea. Three days later, he wrote this story for the introduction:

In the faint light of the attic, an old man, tall and stooped, bent his great frame and made his way to a stack of boxes that sat near one of the little half windows. Brushing aside a wisp of cobwebs, he tilted the top box toward the light and began to carefully lift out one old photograph album after another. Eyes once bright but now dim searched longingly for the source that had drawn him here.

It began with the fond recollection of the love of his life, long gone, and somewhere in these albums was a photo of her he hoped to rediscover. Silent as a mouse, he patiently opened the long-buried treasures and soon was lost in a sea of memories. Although his world had not stopped spinning when his wife left it, the past was more alive in his heart than his present aloneness.

Setting aside one of the dusty albums, he pulled from the box what appeared to be a journal from his grown son's childhood. He could not recall ever having seen it before or that his son had ever kept a journal. *Why did Elizabeth always save the children's old junk?* he wondered, shaking his white head.

Opening the yellowed pages, he glanced over a short entry, and his lips curved in an unconscious smile. Even his eyes brightened as he read the words that spoke clear and sweet to his soul. It was the voice of the little boy who had grown up far too fast, in this very house, and whose voice had grown fainter and fainter over the years. In the utter silence of the attic, the words of a guileless six-year-old worked their magic and carried the old man back to a time almost totally forgotten.

Entry after entry stirred a sentimental hunger in his heart like the longing a gardener feels in the winter for the fragrance of spring flowers. But it was accompanied by the painful memory that his son's simple recollections of those days were far different from his own. But how different?

Reminded that he had kept a daily journal of his business activities over the years, he closed his son's journal, tucked it under his arm, and turned to leave, having forgotten the cherished photo that originally triggered his search. Hunched over to keep from bumping his head on the rafters, the old man stepped to the wooden stairway and made his descent, then headed down a carpeted stairway that led to the den.

Opening a glass cabinet door, he reached in and pulled out an old business journal. Turning, he sat down at his desk and placed the two journals beside each other. His was leather-bound and engraved neatly with his name in gold, while his son's was tattered and the name "Jimmy" had been nearly scuffed from its surface. He ran a long, skinny finger over the letters as though he could restore what had been worn away with time and use.

As he opened his journal, the old man's eyes fell upon an inscription that stood out because it was so brief in comparison to other days. In his own neat handwriting were these words:

Wasted the whole day fishing with Jimmy.
Didn't catch a thing.

With a deep sigh and a shaking hand, he took Jimmy's journal and found the boy's entry for the same day, June 4. Large scrawling letters pressed deeply in the paper read:

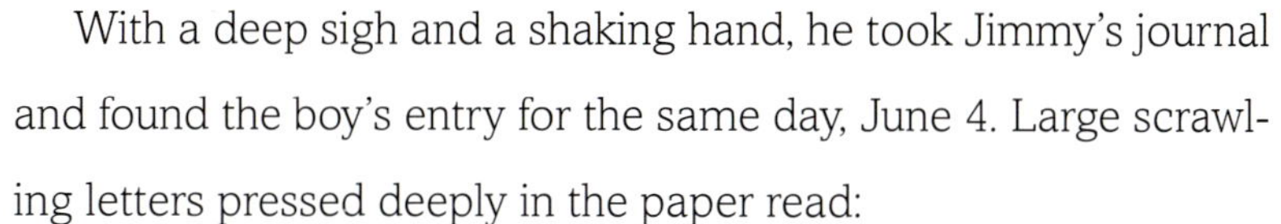

You may have heard a variation of this quote before, but it bears repeating: "I've never known anyone who on their deathbed said, 'I wish I had spent more time at the office.'"

Our Dash is a fleeting moment in time, and what we do with it is up to us. This quote says it all:

A hundred years from now
it will not matter what my bank account was,
the sort of house I lived in,
or the kind of car I drove.
But the world may be different because
I was important in the life of a [child].

The Story Behind "The Dash"

By Linda Ellis

It still amazes me that a simple poem I wrote one afternoon has forever changed my life. It all began when I faxed a copy of this poem to a syndicated radio show in Atlanta. Soon after receiving it, the host of this popular show read it on the air. Little did I know how much my life would change from that day forward. Titled "The Dash," these thirty-six lines have touched millions of lives and have literally taken on a life of their own, traveling all over the globe. I call it "uncomplicated poetry in a complicated world."

People are always asking me what inspired me to write this poem. I believe it was a combination of things in my life at the time. I was working for top executives at a very large and successful corporation. It was a strict company with a tense working environment.

I began to see how the priorities in many lives there had become misaligned. It seemed to me that the bosses were worrying far too much about that which was inconsequential in the scope of life.

Also, resonating in the back of my mind were the words from a letter that had been routed around the office, written by the wife of an employee who knew she was dying. I was so moved that I saved a copy of it and continue to live by its words:

> Regrets? I have a few. Too much worrying. I worried about finding the right husband and having children, being on time, being late and so on. It didn't matter. It all works out and it would have worked out without the worries and the tears.

> If only I would have known then what I know now. But I did and so do you. We're all going to die. Stop worrying and start loving and living.

Her words stuck with me. Her letter made me stop and think,

This is it. This is all we get.

I remember where I was when I first truly realized the significance of the piece that I had written. I was on a business trip in Minnesota, alone in a hotel room. I received an emotional e-mail thanking me for sharing the message of "The Dash" from a student who had recently heard it as part of a memorial gathering for the Columbine High School students. I sat on the bed and cried.

Several years later, I found myself engulfed in the thoughts and feelings created by my own words as I listened to them read aloud, for what seemed like the very first time, at the funeral of my father, my best friend. Never have the words of the poem meant more to me.

From being performed in an elementary school play somewhere in the heartland of America to being part of a state Supreme Court justice's speech, from being printed in best-selling novels to high school yearbooks, "The Dash" has truly affected millions. I may not be able to change the world with these words, but I have certainly been able to influence a portion of it! The poem's words have convinced mothers to spend more time with their children, encouraged fathers to spend more time at home, and reunited long-lost loved ones.

The words have changed attitudes and changed the direction of lives. They have, in their own way, made a difference. I know that writing "The Dash" has changed *my* life. I hope that reading it, in some way, may change yours as well.

Live Your Dash,

Linda Ellis

the dash

by LINDA ELLIS

I read of a man who stood to speak
at the funeral of a friend.
He referred to the dates on her tombstone
from the beginning . . . to the end.
He noted that first came the date of her birth
and spoke of the following date with tears,
but he said what mattered most of all
was the dash between those years.
For that dash represents all the time
that she spent alive on earth,
and now only those who loved her
know what that little line is worth.
For it matters not how much we own,
the cars . . . the house . . . the cash.
What matters most is how we live and love
and how we spend our dash.

So think about this long and hard;
are there things you'd like to change?
For you never know how much time is left
that can still be rearranged.
If we could just slow down enough
to consider what's true and real
and always try to understand
the way other people feel.
And be less quick to anger
and show appreciation more
and love the people in our lives . . .
like we've never loved before.
If we treat each other with respect
and more often wear a smile . . .
remembering that this special dash
might only last a little while.
So when your eulogy is being read,
with your life's actions to rehash,
would you be proud of the things they say
about how you spent your dash?

About the Authors

MAC ANDERSON is the founder of Simple Truths and Successories, Inc., the leader in designing and marketing products for motivation and recognition. These companies, however, are not the first success stories for Mac. He was also the founder and CEO of McCord Travel, the largest travel company in the Midwest, and part owner/VP of sales and marketing for Orval Kent Food Company, the country's largest manufacturer of prepared salads.

His accomplishments in these unrelated industries provide some insight into his passion and leadership skills. He also brings the same passion when he speaks to corporate audiences on a variety of topics, including leadership, motivation, and team building.

Mac has authored and coauthored nearly twenty books, including *You Can't Send a Duck to Eagle School*; *The Nature of Success*; *The Power of Attitude*; *The Essence of Leadership*; *Finding Joy*; *To a Child, Love Is Spelled T-I-M-E*; *212° The Extra Degree*; *Change Is Good . . . You Go First*; and recent releases *What's the Big Idea*; *The Power of Kindness*; *The Road to Happiness*; and *212° Service*. In 2006, he launched Simple Truths, a leading provider of motivational and inspirational content and products that reinforce core values.

LINDA ELLIS started writing poems as a child, a talent inherited from her Irish grandmother. She grew up in Florida and then lived in New York for several years. However, her southern roots kept calling her home so she settled in Georgia where she now lives with her family.

She spent years working in the corporate environment, but after her first poem was shared on a syndicated radio program in 1994, an alternative career began to emerge and she soon came to the realization that her true passion was in creative writing.

Because no promotion or raise received from her boss could ever equal the satisfaction she felt when she would hear from those whose hearts had been touched by her words, she made the decision to leave the corporate world behind to pursue her dream, inspiring others through her writings.

Linda focuses on writing about real life, including all of its joys and sorrows. Thus, as each new phase of her own life is experienced, so are new feelings, thoughts, and ideas that she feels compelled to express through her stories and poems.

Her works have such a wide public appeal that they have been featured in best-selling books, major magazines, and various publications; read on TV and radio stations; carved on tombstones; and even used as needlepoint designs by grandmothers!

She credits the support and encouragement of her family and friends for reaching what she considers true success . . . the opportunity to combine what she loves to do with a way to make a living!

Linda now travels around the country speaking about "The Dash" and other inspirations. If you would like more information about Linda's other written works and/or you would like to book her for a speaking engagement, you can contact her directly at www.lindaellis.net.

Notes

1. Joseph Epstein, *Ambition: The Secret Passion* (New York: E. P. Dutton, 1989), 298.

2. John Blumberg , used with permission.

2. Albert Schweitzer, *Memoirs of Childhood and Youth,* 1924.

3. © Barbara Glanz Communications, Inc., 2003. All rights reserved. Used by permission.